New Brunswick's Covered Bridges

by Helen Coldrick

Edited by Susan A. Webber

Neptune Publishing Company Limited
P.O. Box 6941, Station A
Saint John, New Brunswick
E2L 4S4

Neptune Publishing Company Limited (Canada)

We wish to acknowledge and thank the Department of Municipalities, Culture and Housing for their assistance in this publication.

ISBN 0-9692218-3-5 ISBN 9-7809692218-3-8

Printed in Canada

10 9 8 7 6 5 4

CANAAN RIVER #1 – AARON CLARK

About The Artist

Helen is a self-taught artist who developed her craft through long hours of sketching and painting. The covered bridges of our picture province have often found their way into her work.

After graduating from Salisbury Regional High School in 1956, Helen left her native New Brunswick and headed for the west coast. While raising her family she had the opportunity to travel throughout British Columbia, Alberta, Alaska and the Northwestern United States. The vast and varied landscapes provided inspiration for hours of sketching and painting.

Like many New Brunswickers Helen returned to the place of her birth after more than twenty years away. She settled in Salisbury in 1980 and began to share her expertise with aspiring artists of all ages.

In 1982 Helen's Studio, a craft shop was opened. Here Helen makes and sells crafts in the summer and teaches art classes in the winter. In addition she still finds time to pursue her own artwork. Helen is a member of the Moncton Art Society and exhibits her work at various art shows throughout New Brunswick.

DARLINGS ISLAND (NOT IN SERVICE)

FOREWORD

The purpose of this book is threefold. First it is meant to celebrate New Brunswick's wooden covered bridges by providing for the tourist and the New Brunswicker, an insight into the history, construction, and location of these beautiful structures in our province.

The era of the covered bridge in New Brunswick began around the time of Confederation. The fact that some covered bridges have stood the test of over 100 years of Maritime weather is a tribute to their construction. During the 80 year period in which they were built the original design underwent only a few modifications.

Covered bridges are found in 14 of the 15 counties in New Brunswick. They are absent only in Restigouche county. We will track covered bridges in the province travelling from county to county. Our journey begins with Albert County and ends at York.

Had our journey begun in 1975, we would have described 113 covered bridges in New Brunswick. This brings us to the second purpose of " New Brunswick's Covered Bridges." That is to draw attention to the need to preserve the 64 bridges that remain standing in 2009. These unique examples of the workmanship of our forefathers are an important part of our history and our heritage. The rapid disappearance of these structures must be halted. Perhaps this book will encourage native New Brunswickers to join the visitors to our province in experiencing the almost tangible sense of history of these remarkable bridges.

As the reader travels from county to county in search of covered bridges, the third purpose of these pages is realized. Other historical and cultural attractions found along the way are highlighted. We hope your travels will be enjoyable and that you will go home with an appreciation for New Brunswick's rich heritage.

TURTLE CREEK #4 – PETER JONAH

History of Covered Bridges

Wooden covered bridges date back to the 14th century in Europe. Man has always been somewhat nomadic in search of food. His travels in New Brunswick were by foot or canoe. The province is laced by brooks, streams and rivers which were not always easily traversed. As people settled the land the need for some form of river crossing was born.

Prior to the development of a permanent road system, the first crossings were probably makeshift bridges of logs, rocks or ice. However, as communities were gradually settled and developed, trails were blazed and rough roads were made. Thus more permanent crossings were needed and the bridge evolved. The first crude bridges were just logs supported by beams. The arch was soon developed for the covered bridge to protect the structure from the weather and give the bridge more support. Researchers tell us that the first covered bridges were erected in medieval Europe. Among the earliest examples were those built in Lucerne, Switzerland and Florence, Italy in the fourteenth century. The latter bridge, the Ponte Vecchio or "Old Bridge" is a popular attraction in Florence with its shops selling the famous Italian gold jewelry.

The city of Venice, famous for its waterways, also boasts an ancient covered bridge. The Rialto covered bridge was built in the sixteenth century. Its design made it possible for barges to pass underneath it. It too has shops along its sides.

These early structures made use of the truss in their construction. The truss, although having undergone numerous improvements, continues to be an integral part of the design of covered bridges.

It is believed the covered bridge design came to North America in the 1780's with the arrival of the United Empire Loyalists. With the settlement of the United States and particularly New England, many covered bridges were needed to cross the numerous river systems, tributaries, streams and brooks. Thus with bridge construction came the study of bridge design. The Americans were at the forefront particularly with the development of the truss system.

Around the same time as in New England, covered bridges appeared in the Maritimes with the landing of the Loyalists in the late 18th century. As the settlement of New Brunswick spread, more covered bridges were built. The bridges that are standing today are living examples of the pride of craftsmanship, heritage, engineering and design of our forefathers. The oldest covered bridge standing today was built in or around 1870. One of the last covered bridges to be constructed in New Brunswick by the provincial government was the 60 foot long Shikatehawk River Number 2 (Lockhart Mill) in Kent Parish of Carleton County in 1954. There were hundreds of these wooden structures built in the early 20th century in New Brunswick, but today only 64 remain.

They were essential for transportation and commerce. Even today travellers depend on covered bridges to cross several of our waterways.

BAMFORD COLPITTS BRIDGE – COVERDALE RIVER #3

Albert County Covered Bridges

Travellers entering the county of Albert off Route 1 via Route 114 near Sussex, or coming down Route 114 from Moncton should visit Fundy National Park with its campsites and many hiking trails; Hopewell Cape with its famous rocks; the Hillsborough train station; and the nine small covered bridges in this county.

Albert County with its rugged coast borders on the Bay of Fundy and Chignecto Bay to the south, and the Northumberland Strait to the north. Camping in Fundy National Park is ideal in the summer with the freshness of the sea breeze blowing off the Fundy coast.

There are two covered bridges in Fundy National Park. The dramatic red structure at Point Wolfe received national attention when it collapsed in 1990. Through efforts by the Albert County Historical Society this popular bridge was rebuilt in 1992.

The other covered bridge in the park is still standing on Barrett Road near the park's boundary. Known as the Lower Forty-Five, the bridge is off the beaten track but worth the journey. It stretches above the depths of a ravine that cuts a path through the rugged forest. Rising from the ravine is the rushing sound of a stream far below.

Locals refer to the William Mitton covered bridge, near Riverview, as the "travelling bridge." The reference is not to the ability to cross Turtle Creek, instead the name reminds us that the bridge was moved from Kent County to its present location. It is one of only a few New Brunswick covered bridges with Burr trusses as opposed to the more traditional Howe truss design.

If one were to follow Turtle Creek to its origin, the Peter Jonah covered bridge would be seen. This bridge is 64 feet long and has one of the cottage type roofs.

The Coverdale River, previously known as the Little River, has one covered bridge structure crossing it. It is the Bamford Colpitts Bridge at Colpitts Settlement. From this bridge one often sees cows grazing nearby drinking the water beneath it, or simply using the bridge for its shade against the hot summer sun.

POINT WOLFE

The Germantown Bridge, the Sawmill Creek Bridge and the Crooked Creek Bridge are all near Route 114. All are worth exploring. Many worn trails lead to the stream running underneath the Germantown Bridge in this marshy area providing an indication of its reputation as a favourite fishing hole. Sawmill Creek 0.5 at Hopewell Hill is not in service but can be seen from Route 114. Crooked Creek Bridge is quite a ways in the rugged Lumsden Road near the town of Albert. It is a simple rustic bridge with a gravelled road entrance set deep in the woods.

On Route 910 is the last bridge in Albert County. The Hartley Steeves Bridge is a quaint small structure that now stands alone. The Harris Steeves Bridge stood within 30 to 40 metres of its shorter neighbour. It was badly damaged when struck by a snowplough in February of 1989. This incident destroyed the bridge.The Hartley Steeves Bridge is a physical reminder of a bit of New Brunswick's folklore. Legend had it that a young engineer involved in the construction of the Bridge fell in love with a local girl and married her. Their romance was remembered by the nickname given to the structure, the "Dan Cupid Bridge".

LOWER FORTY – FIVE #1

Carleton County Covered Bridges

Carleton County boasts the longest covered bridge in the world, the Hartland Bridge. This world famous attraction crosses the Saint John River at Hartland. It is 391 metres or 1282 feet in length. The original Hartland Bridge was constructed in 1901 by the privately owned Hartland Toll Bridge Company. There were seven truss spans, five 167'6" in length, and two 144' in length. The chords were made of British Columbia Douglas Fir and the floor beams of New Brunswick Black Spruce. In 1921 most of the bridge was replaced. The wooden piers and abutments were replaced with reinforced concrete. The original spans were Howe trusses and were covered in 1924. In 1944 the Bridge Department dismantled the original stone filled cribwork approach at the village end of the bridge and rebuilt a new approach consisting of reinforced concrete trestle beds and slab spans.

The Saint John River flows through Carleton County's rich farmland where it is joined on the western side by the Presquile, River de Chute and further south at Woodstock by the Meduxnekeag. A bridge crossing the Meduxenekeag near Weston close to the Maine border, was torn down in the early 1990s. This was unfortunate because the caution signs on the bridge had been unique. They were not the regular yellow and black ones from the Department of Public Works, but were the unique hand-painted ones of black and white.

On the eastern side of the Saint John River, there are three streams named the Becaguimec, Shikatehawk, and Monquart with the towns of Hartland, Bristol, and Bath at their entrances to the Saint John. There are three covered bridges crossing the Becaguimec. All three are at Brighton. The Adair and Ellis Bridges are both short, being under 70 feet in length. The Mangrum Bridge is longer and was built in the same year as the Ellis Bridge in 1909. The Keenan covered bridge crossing the Monquart at Kent was recently destroyed by fire. All three of these sturdy structures are worth exploring. It should be noted that all of this back country is beautiful, especially in the fall when the leaves change colour, so bring a camera.

FLORENCEVILLE BRIDGE

The bridge at Lockhart Mill on the Shikatehawk no longer stands. It used to bear an interesting sign which warned that a 20 dollar fine would be levied for driving any animal faster than a walk across the bridge.

Florenceville is the home of the fifth covered bridge in the county. It is an unusual combination of several steel truss spans and one covered bridge span. It was built in 1907 and is 950 feet in length with one covered span being 154 feet long. It can be viewed at a distance from the old Trans Canada Highway but this vantage point does not do it justice. It is well worth travelling along the winding road to the structure and journeying through the narrow span.

This county is another must for covered bridge explorers who will also enjoy the beautiful setting of rich farmland and peaceful rivers. This is "Potato Country", home of the world famous McCain frozen food industries.

HARTLAND BRIDGE

Charlotte County Covered Bridges

Charlotte County, in the southwestern corner of New Brunswick has seven covered bridges still standing. It is the first county you enter travelling north from Maine, U.S.A. crossing the St. Croix River to St. Stephen, New Brunswick, Canada. The first covered bridge is only a few kilometres away at Maxwell Crossing where it spans Dennis Stream. This small covered bridge is only 60 feet long. Its cedar shingled roof has been replaced with sheets of steel.

The town of St. Stephen is the largest in Charlotte County. It is home to the Ganong Chocolate Factory. This firm made the world's first chocolate bar in 1906. On Main Street is the Chocolatier Shop, a testament to the wide selection of famous Ganong chocolates. The town also hosts a Chocolate Fest in August of every year which will delight chocolate lovers of all ages.

Travelling up Route 1 approximately 15 miles from St. Stephen, you come to Route 760. Following the paved road you come across three covered bridges in a circuit. These bridges all span the Digdeguash River which flows through the county and enters the Passamaquoddy Bay through Digdeguash Bay. The three bridges are called the McGuire, the McCann, and the Dumbarton. Built in the early 1900's all of these bridges are similar in construction and size. They all have large granite abutments and similar size openings and carrying capacity.

After viewing the covered bridges on Route 760 take time to visit the famous seaside town of St. Andrews. Located off Route 1 on Route 127, St. Andrews is a major summer resort town popular with wealthy Canadians and Americans. Picturesque in both summer and fall, the town offers waterfront restaurants, antique shops, an ocean front golf course, the Ross Memorial Museum, the St. Andrews Blockhouse, the Algonquin Hotel and much more. St. Andrews was founded in 1783 by American Loyalists emigrating from New England. A dominant feature in St. Andrews is the famous Algonquin Hotel, built in the 1800's by Canadian railway magnate, William Van Horne.

St. Andrews is also the site of the internationally respected Huntsman Marine Laboratory and Aquarium. Scientific research on the marine ecology of the Bay of Fundy is carried out there and you can visit the aquarium to see the various types of marine life which live in the Bay of Fundy.

Leaving St. Andrews and continuing north on Route 1, we come to the town of St. George. Here on the outskirts of the town in a rural setting is the Canal Covered Bridge crossing the Canal Stream. The bridge was built in 1917. Like all of New Brunswick's covered bridges, it has a weathered grey look.

DIGDEGUASH RIVER #4 – MCCANN

In the northern section of the county, near the origin of the Magaguadavic River, which runs down the middle of the county, is the Flume Ridge Covered Bridge on Clark's Mill Pond Road. It is reinforced with a steel framework and was built using the Burr truss design. It is also a delight for the swimmer with a love of adventure for a swinging rope hangs from the bottom of the bridge overhanging the deep gullies of fresh water.

Following up Route 1 to Saint John you pass Pennfield Ridge in the heart of blueberry country with U-Pick locations available in August. Near Lepreau down Route 790 to the Fundy Coast you can pick clams, periwinkles, or go deep sea fishing. There are also scenic coastal excursions that can be arranged with Fundy Yachts. One can also tour the communities of Musquash, Chance Harbour, Dipper Harbour, Beaver Harbour, and Black's Harbour where you may pick up some fresh fish, lobster, oysters and various other marine products. New River Beach just off Route 1, 25 minutes from Saint John, is an excellent spot for a picnic. Swimming is restricted to the very hardiest of individuals while most bathers stick to wading along the sandy shoreline. After lunch you might walk along the beach to Haggerty's Cove where you can pick up a well maintained trail that follows the shoreline in and out of the forest.

Charlotte County is also famous for the three Fundy Islands located in the Bay of Fundy. Grand Manan is the largest and is well known for its birds, porpoise, seal, and whale watching. Locals provide whaling trips for close-up camera shots of the mammals. A trip to visit the Puffins is also worthwhile. Grand Manan is also noted for the harvest of the marine delicacy, dulse. Visitors claim that this is an acquired taste!

The last bridge in Charlotte County is found near the outskirts of Saint John. Unfortunately, the Mill Pond Bridge at Little Lepreau is no longer a part of the road system. Still accessible by foot, the covered bridge enthusiast may want to explore its crooks and crannies.

Gloucester County Covered Bridges

There is only one covered bridge in Gloucester County. It is a replica built in the Acadian Historical Village near Bertrand. This authentic historical site is an interesting place to visit. It portrays the live of Acadians between 1770 and 1949. The more than 40 complexes are staffed by interpreters who bring back to life ancestral customs and the traditional trader lifestyle.

MAGAGUADAVIC RIVER #7 – FLUME RIDGE

Kent County Covered Bridges

Kent County is located in central eastern New Brunswick above Westmorland County and bordering on the Northumberland Strait. It is dotted with quiet, quaint villages and an abundance of lovely rivers. Famous industrialist K.C. Irving was born in this county in the village of Bouctouche. There are two covered bridges left standing in the county.

Many of the people who live in Kent County are French and descend from the original Acadian settlers. Fishing is the main industry.

This county is also the location of Kouchibouquac National Park with its ninety-three square miles of nature trails in the summer and cross-country ski trails in the winter. The park is noted for its interesting geography and its beautiful long sandy beaches bordered by sand dunes.

Many of the settlements in Kent County are at the river's mouth, near the coast. On entering the county from Westmorland, you come first to a town, bay, and river all bearing the French name Cocagne. On this river at Notre Dame was once a magnificent bridge. It has been replaced by a modern structure with greater carrying capacity.

Richibucto is the largest town in the county. Again there is a town, bay and river with the same name. The Richibucto River has several tributaries flowing from it, one of which bears a covered bridge. The Tom Graham Bridge spans Graham Creek while a second one, recently lost to fire, crossed the St. Nicholas River. This covered bridge was at the mouth of the St. Nicholas River and it was a beauty. It was one of the longest covered bridges in the province at 502 feet and was comprised of three long spans. The bridge also had 12 square windows running its length. Unfortunately, the smaller covered bridge at Rexton that crossed the St. Nicholas River where it narrows was also destroyed by fire.

Travelling north and inland on the Kouchibouguacis River one will find a covered bridge at Camerons Mill. This lovely bridge was built relatively recently in 1950 and spans the river over 200 feet.

With its numerous rivers, one might expect to find several covered bridges in Kent County. Unfortunately, the need for bridges with greater carrying capacity evolved as car and truck traffic increased. As in other counties, many of the covered bridges fell into disrepair, were abandoned and eventually collapsed or were dismantled. Today only two are left to explôre, but these are still worth the trip.

ST. NICHOLAS RIVER #1 – MOUTH (NOT STANDING)

Kings County Covered Bridges

Kings County is touted as the "Covered Bridge Capital of The World" and it may very well be. There are sixteen covered bridges in this county. If your time is limited, you should begin your journey here.

The meeting of the Saint John River, the Kennebecasis River and Belleisle Creek forms the lush and lovely Kingston Peninsula. The peninsula can be reached off Route 7 west of Saint John crossing by ferry at Westfield to Harding's Point or travelling east of the city along Route 100 crossing at Gondola Point. The Kingston Peninsula has several historical reminders including Trinity Anglican Church (a National Historic Site) and the John Fischer Museum. The Saturday morning farmer's market, also at Kingston, is reminiscent of bygone days. On this peninsula there used to be several covered bridges, but today only one remains. This is the Bayswater Bridge on Route 845 at Bayswater. It consists of two spans and is supported by two abutments and a pier in the center as it crosses Milkish Inlet.

The 71 foot Marven Bridge, off Route 124 on Swamp Road crosses Belleisle Creek at Springfield. It was erected in 1903. Nearby is Marven Park with its picnic area.

The Hammond River, which meets the Kennebecasis River near the village of Nauwigewauk is spanned by three covered bridges. The most picturesque of these joins nearby Darlings Island to the mainland. It is not in service.

One must follow the twists and turns of the Hammond River through the marshy flatland to fully appreciate the beauty of the countryside. The area has plenty of ducks, other waterfowl, and fish for the wildlife enthusiast.

Route 860 follows the Hammond River as it winds through lush meadows leading us on to two more covered bridges, one at Smithstown and the other at French Village. From these bridges one overlooks favourite local swimming and fishing holes. The speckled trout and silver salmon harbour beneath in the fresh water waiting for the willing angler.

Route 1 follows along the Kennebecasis River eastward. Approximately 15 miles (24 kms.) before reaching Sussex an iron bridge and a covered bridge can be seen from the highway at Bloomfield. A little further on the Moosehorn Bridge stands on an abandoned stretch of road running beside Route 1 just before the Norton turnoff. This bridge still has its original cedar shingled roof.

Surrounding the town of Sussex are the remaining nine bridges in Kings County. Sussex is the dairy capital of New Brunswick. It is known for its rolling pastures, friendly people, and fertile land. Barbour's Foods is one of the oldest businesses of this dairy town. Sussex was also once the main military compound for our militia. Today it still has an Armoury and rifle range although the range is not used for training.

HAMMOND RIVER #3 – SMITHTOWN

Southeast on Route 121 to Waterford towards the ski resort at Poley Mountain, are two wooden covered bridges, each similar in structure and size, crossing Trout Creek.

On Waterford Road nearer to Poley Mountain is Urney Bridge (Trout Creek Number Four). The Urney Bridge is 66 feet long and was built in 1905. Just past Poley Mountain is Moores Mills Bridge (Trout Creek Number Five) on Drummond Road off Route 121. Still in service this bridge has a carrying capacity of up to 15 tons and is only slightly shorter than the other bridge at 58 feet 6 inches. Its weathered grey look blends in with the surrounding picturesque setting. This is breathtakingly beautiful country so pack a lunch for your trip and load your camera.

The Malone Bridge located on Goshen Road off Route 114 is a lovely bridge in a picturesque setting. In the background is a farm with cows grazing nearby. The Centreville Bridge on Pleasant Ridge Branch Road, just off Route 880 at Berwick is located in the Parish of Studholm. It still has its original cedar shingled roof. The Tranton Bridge off Route 890 on Roachville Road is surrounded by farmers' fields. This bridge has had its original cedar shingled roof replaced with a sheet metal roof like most of the bridges in Kings County. The Salmon River Bridge is a quaint structure.

The bridge is just off Route 890 and is not in service. The Plumweseep bridge is on Plumweseep Road just off the Route 1 heading to Moncton. This bridge was built in 1911 according to the inscription above its entrance. There are numerous gaps in the sidings of this bridge. The other remaining bridge in Kings County is the MacFarlane Bridge. It is located off Route 111 on Wards Creek Road and was built with the Howe truss design like all the covered bridges left standing in Kings County. This bridge has a recommended carrying capacity of between a minimum six and a maximum eight tonnes axle.

OLDFIELDS – SMITH CREEK #5

Madawaska County Covered Bridges

Madawaska County is nestled in the northwest corner of New Brunswick, bordering on the State of Maine, U.S.A. to the southwest and Quebec to the north. It is here in Madawaska that the Saint John River begins its long journey towards the Bay of Fundy. As it travels south, it is soon joined by several streams including the Madawaska, the Iroquois, the Quisibis, the Riviere Verte and Baker Brook.

The largest city in Madawaska is Edmundston, a French speaking town of 17,000 people. The large Fraser interests provide most of the employment in the area via the forestry sector. The people of Madawaska are primarily a blend of Acadians, Indians, English, and Quebec French but there is no doubt the heart and soul of Madawaska is definitely French and Catholic. The elegant churches majestically standing tall on their riverbanks attest to this as well as to the fine craftsmanship of the time.

There are three covered bridges in the county. Baker Brook Number Two Bridge on Cyr Street near Route 120 crosses the brook it is named after. Boniface Bridge spans the Green River (Riviere Verte) at St. Basile. It is a nice structure.

The Quisibis River Number Two covered bridge crosses the river that bears its name. It is a short bridge only 55 feet and 4 inches long. The Madawaska County covered bridges were all built in the 20th century between 1925 and 1951.

IROQUOIS RIVER #4 (NOT STANDING)

Northumberland County Covered Bridges

Northumberland County is made famous by the river that begins its course inland near Chatham and Newcastle and soon splits into the Northwest Miramichi and the Southwest Miramichi. So dominant is this river that much of the area surrounding it is commonly referred to as the Miramichi.

The fame of this great river is known internationally. Movie stars and others come here to fish for the Atlantic Salmon.

The Salmon Museum at Doaktown traces the life cycle of the salmon providing a greater appreciation of the beauty of this fish. The visitor will enjoy viewing the salmon close up in the holding tanks.

Another small town on the Miramichi is Boiestown, home to the Woodmen's Museum. Those interested in nature and lumbering will be sure to enjoy a trip through this museum.

Folk legends abound on the Miramichi. This is a region that has been home to generations of families providing a sense of continuity so typical of small towns. Each generation has passed on the folklore of the Miramichi in stories and songs. Those lucky enough to be in Newcastle in August may participate in this sharing of culture as the town hosts the famous Miramichi Folk Song Festival. Irish from far and wide converge on neighboring Chatham in July to celebrate their heritage. This annual festival in green provides activities and events to please young and old alike.

Northumberland County provides further evidence of the demise of the covered bridge. The Miramichi, Tabusintac and Napan Rivers and their tributaries figured largely in the history of the region with communities facing each other across these watery divides. Thus covered bridges were constructed in numerous locations along these waterways.

Today only a single covered bridge remains at Nelson Hollow near the Miramichi just off Route 8. Built in 1900, the bridge is no longer in use today. It is the oldest covered bridge in New Brunswick. In 1938 it was replaced by a steel bridge nearby. In 1971 this bridge was replaced with another bridge with structural plate pipes.

In 1977 the Doaktown Historical Society recognized the value of this structure and restored it. The bridge is unique in the province in its use of the Town Lattice truss design. Also of interest is its Hansard type roof. It is a fine example of the excellent craftsmanship of our ancestors.

NELSON HOLLOW BRIDGE

Queens County Covered Bridges

Queens County is located just above Kings County in south central New Brunswick. It has some beautiful back country and possesses some extensive water systems. These include Grand Lake, the largest in New Brunswick; the Washademoak Lake and numerous smaller lakes, rivers and tributaries. Both Grand Lake and the Washademoak are recreational areas reknowned for excellent swimming, sailing, and boating. In the summer the surrounding cottages spring to life as families converge for fun and recreation.

The Saint John River, dotted with islands, widens as it journeys through Queens County. Among the other waterways in the county are the Nerepis River to the south, the Canaan which flows into the Washademoak and the Salmon and Gaspereau Rivers which flow into Grand Lake. The six mile long Jemseg River connects Grand Lake with the Saint John River. The area close to the Saint John River is notable for its elm trees, fertile farmland, and fine hayland. This area also provides excellent hunting and fishing for the avid sportsman.

The Nerepis River cuts a narrow path through the hills allowing only the railway to pass near the stream. The highway leads the traveller over the hill to a lovely little valley where the village of Welsford is nestled surrounded by hills. Sadly the Nerepis River Number Three was lost due to flooding. This leaves us with 3 covered bridges in the county.

The Burpee Covered Bridge traverses the Gaspereau River just a few miles from the town of Chipman in a section of thick forest. Built in 1913 in this heavily forested land, it was named in honour of a family which lived nearby. Those who enjoy unspoiled natural beauty will be glad they took the time to visit this isolated but magnificant area.

The two other covered bridges in the county are the Clark Aaron Bridge and the Starkey Bridge. The Clark Aaron Bridge spans the Canaan River on the Cherryvale Road while the Starkey Bridge (Long Creek Number One) spans Long Creek where it flows into the Canaan River. Built in 1939, this bridge is still used and the road to the entrance has been upgraded to present-day standards.

FORKS BRIDGE (NOT STANDING) P.A.N.B.

Saint John County Covered Bridges

Saint John County is a narrow strip of land bordering the Bay of Fundy in central southern New Brunswick. New Brunswick's largest city, Saint John (population 125,000 metro) is located at the mouth of the Saint John River which runs inland 425 miles through New Brunswick to its headwaters in Northern Maine. It is at the mouth of the river that the World Famous Reversing Falls Rapids may be observed. It is a natural phenomenon created by the meeting of the waters of the Bay of Fundy and the Saint John River.

In the Bay of Fundy are found the "highest tides in the world," and it is this tidal action which creates the rapids. During the reversing cycle, the tides gradually cause the river to stop flowing downstream; the river turns back on itself and flows upriver.

At low tide the river runs downstream, thundering through the narrow gorge under the highway and rail bridges and into the harbour. This creates white water rapids and whirlpools. From low tide the waters of the Bay gradually rise until they come even to the height of the river water. At this point, which is called "slack tide", the rapids are calmed.

As the Bay water continues to rise, the flow of the river again reverses because the Bay water is now higher than the river level. At high tide, the current is once again running upstream. The entire reversing process covers a 12 hour period.

Saint John has much to offer its visitors. Those with an interest in history will find much to occupy their time but to explore the three covered bridges in the county we must travel away from the city. Following Loch Lomond Road east on Route 111, we pass the Saint John Airport. As you turn right past the Loch Lomond Lakes, take the next right hand turn on Route 825 towards Black River, Gardners Creek, and Tynemouth Creek. At the mouth of Tynemouth Creek is a covered bridge. Here there is a breathtaking view of the marshland and ocean in the distance. With or without a camera, this scene creates a lasting impression. Joining back on Route 111 ten minutes later we come to the quiet seaside village of St. Martins famous for its caves. Forty-five kilometres (27 miles) east of Saint John this village is charming with its older homes, cottages, and two wooden covered bridges. The Hardscrabble and Vaughan Creek Number One are in close proximity to each other. The Hardscrabble Bridge crosses Vaughan Creek. Vaughan Creek Number One Bridge crosses Irish River and has an attached closed-in walkway with a sloped roof and windows to look through to view the Bay of Fundy. Nearby is a lighthouse and wharf.

St. Martins was once an active shipbuilding community but today it is a quiet community with an active fishing fleet. It is a popular spot for the vacationer looking for a unique and memorable experience.

TYNEMOUTH CREEK BRIDGE

Sunbury County Covered Bridges

At one time Sunbury County comprised all of New Brunswick and formed a part of Nova Scotia. Today, Sunbury County is rather small in area and is sandwiched between York and Queens Counties. This flat and fertile land is excellent for farming. Unfortunately, it also lies very low so each spring the Saint John River overflows its banks covering surrounding fields and even the highway! When the water subsides, the land is planted and vegetables flourish in the rich soil left behind.

Sunbury County has four covered bridges still standing. There are two covered bridges on the South Oromocto River, the Mill Settlement Bridge and the Bell Bridge. Both bridges have concrete abutments and are similar in size and length. If you look closely at the Bell Bridge, you will notice under the eaves tiny square holes at regular intervals. These holes were used to support scaffolding when repairs were made to the bridge.

The Back Creek Covered Bridge on Hoyt Station Road crosses the creek for which it is named. This is approximately 94 feet in length crossing a seemingly quiet brook except in springtime when its flood waters threaten the wooden structure. You should note the fencing nearby. It is a good example of the log fences built in the early 20th century.

The covered bridge which may be most pleasing in the county is the Patrick Owens Bridge which crosses the Rusagonis River at Lincoln. This bridge is 115 feet 6 inches long and is comprised of two spans. It has a roofed window almost the complete length of the structure which provides an interesting lighting effect. Plan to spend some time at the picnic area at one end of the bridge. Later you may want to visit the nearby Pioneer Cemetery. At the other end of the bridge stands an elegant home which was built as a stopover for the stagecoach that travelled between St. Stephen and Fredericton.

SOUTH OROMOCTO RIVER #2

Victoria County Covered Bridges

In Victoria County only one covered bridge has survived. This picturesque covered bridge crosses the Odellach River near Arthurette on Route 109. Known as the Tomlinson Mill Bridge, it was erected in 1918 and is 60 feet long with canopied windows on either side. Nearby is a lumber mill which is in and out of operation depending on market conditions.

Victoria County is sparsely populated. It borders on the State of Maine just below Madawaska County. The traveller may be surprised to see barns with only their roofs protruding from the ground. This is a sign that the potato belt has begun. These barns are designed to provide insulation and proper temperature for stored potato crops.

The Saint John River flows through Victoria County and is intersected by the Aroostook and Tobique Rivers. The Aroostook flows through a series of rolling hills and valleys into Maine. The Tobique is a fast flowing river system in itself. It narrows in many places as it courses between steep cliffs and forms rapids at its mouth. Its tributaries come close to other rivers but they are narrow and shallow and not convenient for travelling. The Odellach River spanned by the last remaining covered bridge is one of the waterways flowing into the Tobique.

ODELLACH RIVER #2 – TOMLINSON MILL

Westmorland County Bridges

Westmorland County in the southeast corner of New Brunswick borders Nova Scotia. An iron bridge over the Missaguash River joins the two provinces while the Petitcodiac River divides Westmorland from Albert County. The Petitcodiac is known for the daily natural phenomenon called the Fundy Tidal Bore on the Petitcodiac River.

The people who live in the county are predominantly a mixture of Acadians and English. Farming and fishing are the basic industries except in Moncton, a fast growing city with a population of 115,000. It is the transportation hub of the Maritimes and is popular for its shopping and nightly entertainment. It has become a center for sporting events and music concerts.

Nearby is Shediac with Parlee Beach, a warm sandy beach on the Northumberland Strait. The Annual Lobster Festival brings many tourists to the town for a week long celebration of food and fun. Travellers may want to stop at nearby Magnetic Hill to witness an illusion of gravity being defied as you drive down the hill. From here you will want to take the children to Magic Mountain for fun on the water slides or to Dieppe to the Crystal Palace, a children's amusement center, before travelling on to see the wooden bridges in Westmorland County.

The county is interspersed with seven covered bridges. One crosses the Petitcodiac River close to the village of Salisbury. Named the Hasty Bridge, it is 123 feet 4 inches long and was built in 1929.

Next is a quaint little covered bridge on the Shediac River. It bears the name of Joshua Gallant, one of the early settlers of the area. It is located on the Shediac River Road. This bridge is closed to traffic.

Crossing the Cocagne River near Moncton are two covered bridges, the Poirier and the Budd Bridges. The Poirier Bridge has undergone repairs. A relatively long covered bridge, it is 136 feet in length. It has had most of its sidings replaced. The Budd Bridge is shorter (83 feet in length) and was built in 1913 by a local contractor.

There is a relocated bridge leading to Magnetic Hill. It was originally the Parkingdale Bridge, named after a school teacher. Built in 1915, it spanned the Coverdale River. Later it was dismantled and relocated to the Magnetic Hill Zoo and Game Farm in Moncton. The reconstruction was supervised and completed in 1983 by Austin Renton of Lower Coverdale. Mr. Renton was an enthusiastic employee of the Bridge Department who for years worked feverishly in the upkeep of many of the Albert and Westmorland covered bridges. The other 2 covered bridges in the county are the Memramcook No.4 located off Gayton Road and built in 1930 and the Tantramar River No.2 located near Sackville and built in 1916.

SHEDIAC RIVER #4

York County Covered Bridges

York County is the home of New Brunswick's capital city, Fredericton with a metropolitan population of 90,000. Its residents include mostly government workers and those engaged at New Brunswick's largest post-secondary institution, the University of New Brunswick. Some of the tourist attractions in the city include Christ Church Cathedral, the Legislative Buildings, and the York Sunbury Historical Society Museum.

There are also numerous lakes and rivers in this county. At nearby Mactaquac, the headpond is an ideal place for fishing, sailing, and swimming. Just beyond Mactaquac following Route 104 is the agricultural area of Keswick. Two covered bridges in York County used to span the scenic Keswick River, one of which was called the Stone Ridge Bridge. This quaint structure was 123 feet 4 inches long and was constructed in 1914. It recently burned to the ground. Another bridge crossing the Keswick was also lost to fire. Built in 1899, the Burnside-Haynes was one of the oldest covered bridges in New Brunswick. It was built at Bright and Douglas and was of the Burr truss design. This structure was unique with its slanted ends and shingled roof.

For winter ski enthusiasts, further out Route 104 , about a 45 minute drive from Fredericton, is Crabbe Mountain Ski Resort near Upper Hainesville. The mountain has trails for the beginner and expert alike.

The Eel River bears the first of York Counties two bridges. Found on the south side of the Saint John River, the Eel forms part of the boundary between York and Carleton Counties. The tiny settlement of Benton is the only village along this river. It is the site of the 104 foot 6 inches Benton Bridge. Near this rather rustic, but delightful span, is a picnic park complete with a memorial to Milton Gregg. Mr. Gregg was a distinguished gentleman who was an advocate for the preservation of New Brunswick's Covered Bridges.

To locate the second covered bridge in the county, one could follow the railway tracks to Nackawic Siding. Nearby is the Nackawic Siding Covered Bridge on the Nackawic Siding Road between Nackawic and Nortondale. This bridge is quite isolated. The roadway leading to the crossing is rough and may be best accessed by a four wheel drive.

EEL RIVER #3

CONSTRUCTION

Trusses

The truss is the fundamental rudiment in the structural framework of the covered bridge. It made use of the amazing triangle for strength, rigidity and the distribution of weight. The form of a triangle cannot be altered. Even under stress, a triangle will resist until it is broken making it far superior to the less rigid rectangle for bridge construction.

The first known truss designed in covered bridges was the "King Post". It was simply a triangle. Although it was strong it was limited in that it could only be used for very short bridges. When a triangle was placed at each end of a rectangle, greater stability was achieved thus allowing the bridge to span a much greater distance. This modification was named the "Queen" truss.

When the bridge construction design moved to North America, many American builders patented their own variations of the wooden truss. Theodore Burr's addition of an arch to the King Post truss was popular in New England. This design can be seen in some of the bridges remaining in New Brunswick today.

Ithiel Town, another American, developed a truss which took the form of a lattice through the use of timbers pegged together. This ingenious design took advantage of the weight of vehicles on the floor of the bridge to automatically tighten the framework. It was a design patented in 1820 and used by many North American building contractors. The Nelson Hollow Bridge in Northumberland County is the only structure in the province which employs this design.

Another important invention in covered bridge construction was William Howe's employment of steel or iron rods to supplement the wooden truss. These rods had swollen threaded ends with nuts attached that could be tightened or loosened, thus tightening or loosening the rods. If a bridge began to sag the problem could easily be rectified in this way. The Howe truss design is seen in most of the covered bridges still standing in New Brunswick today.

RUSAGONIS RIVER #2 – PATRICK OWENS

Abutments

An abutment is a support at the end of a truss. Most of New Brunswick's covered bridges are a single span which reaches from one abutment to another. A wider waterway required several spans. These spans rest on concrete piers in addition to the abutments. The Hartland Bridge has seven spans, five 167'6" in length, and two 144' in length resting on six piers.

The annual spring thaw with its inevitable ice jams necessitated the development of "ice-breakers" pointing upstream to help break up the ice jams, thus protecting the piers. The piers were also pointed to help preserve the wooden covered bridges from being washed out in both spring floods and heavy rains.

Abutments supporting the first bridges were made of large hewn stones or log cribs filled with stones. Sometimes closed-in timber cribs of hemlock or spruce were used running crossways in a bank at either end of the covered bridge. Later on many of the abutments were replaced with poured concrete.

The ramps which join roadways to bridge entrances are constructed on a base of rocks or field stones making good drainage possible. Some of these ramps are like artwork with layers of flat stones placed in interwoven patterns and wrapped in chicken wire. Many exhibit the fine handiwork of proficient workmen and are intact even today. Some of the ramps also included wooden platforms and guardrails. Most of these have been destroyed and the roads leading up to the entrances have been chip sealed for greater carrying capacity and safety.

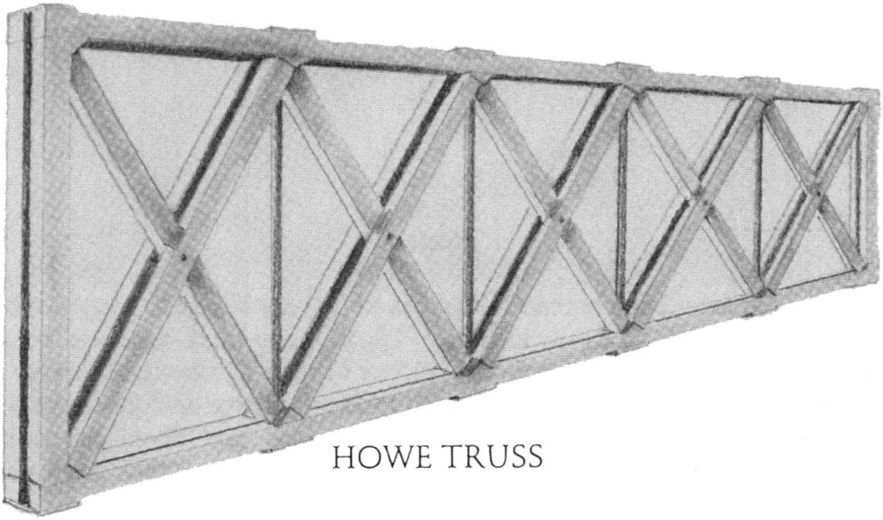

HOWE TRUSS

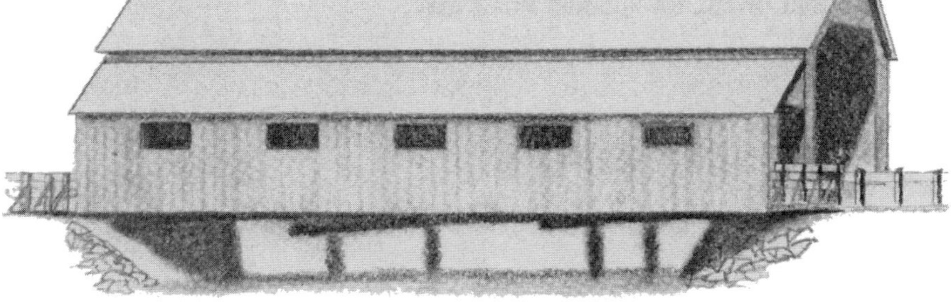

COVERED WALKWAY – VAUGHAN CREEK #1

Bases

The base of a covered bridge has to be very strong to carry weights of up to 15 tonnes from truck traffic. Usually, any truck over this weight would not be permitted to cross the bridges for fear of structural damage to the bridge. The bases were constructed of heavy chords and crossbeams of solid timber. These were joined by steel rods and rested on timber projections, called corbels, on each abutment. The heavy chords were made of imported Douglas fir or white pine. Spruce or elm stringers were placed over the base lengthwise and then a subfloor of boards, usually New Brunswick black spruce, was laid diagonally. This design contributed to the stability of the whole structure. Finally, over all of this the planking of the deck was placed. Typically, the planks were laid lengthwise, but in New Brunswick you will also see covered bridge floors laid crosswise, diagonally or in a more interesting herringbone pattern.

Most of the floors laid in New Brunswick's covered bridges built in the late 1800's or early 1900's are made of softwood black spruce. After 1940, the treated hardwoods, maple or yellow birch, replaced black spruce for flooring. These woods were usually chemically treated with the wood preservatives creosote or pentox. These were effective in achieving water resistance and protected against wood rot.

CHORD & CROSSBEAM – IROQUOIS RIVER #4
(NOT STANDING)

SMITH CREEK #5 – OLDFIELDS

Sidings

The outside covering of the frame of the covered bridge was usually done with rough hemlock boards. These boards were attached vertically to the trusses usually in one piece and in varying lengths. These boards aged over the years to a grey or pewter-like colour. Most of New Brunswick's covered bridges standing today are this colour.

New Brunswick only had a few covered bridges that were painted and the last one, a striking red one at Point Wolfe in Fundy National Park collapsed in 1990. However, this bridge has been rebuilt and reopened in June of 1992.

The sight of a short row of side boards at the bottom of a covered bridge is evidence that the lower chords have been repaired.

TANTRAMAR RIVER #2 – SACKVILLE

Entrances

Every covered bridge in New Brunswick has two open ends to serve as entrances and exits. However, not all of New Brunswick's covered bridge entrances are serviceable. Salmon River, Darlings Island and Moosehorn Bri--dges in Kings County and the Sawmill Creek Number One in Albert County are examples of the bridges that are closed to vehicular traffic.

The height of most entrances in New Brunswick's covered bridges range from 3.4 metres to 4.2 metres and widths of 2.8 metres to 3.2 metres. The openings of New Brunswick bridges come in a variety of shapes from square to almost perfectly rounded arches. The Patrick Owens Bridge in Sunbury County or the William Mitton Bridge in Albert County have square openings, while the Hartland Bridge in Carleton County has a rounded archway. Most of New Brunswick bridge entranceways are neither square or round, but something in between, similar to an oval.

Above the entranceway is usually an inscription of the name of the bridge, the date it was built, and sometimes the carrying capacity. Most of our covered bridges can carry vehicles ranging in weight from six to fifteen tonnes. It is important for drivers of commerical vehicles to follow these signs for safety reasons. Undue stress on the bridge floor can result in permanent structural damage or collapse.

A covered bridge provides refuge from rain or the hot sun in summer, brisk wind in fall, and sleet and snow in winter. The aura of bridges and their dark openings can stir feelings of uncertainty, mystery, or romance. Once inside a covered bridge, there is no door to close behind you. A glance between the open sidings or out a window can provide a lasting picture of the beautiful landscape beyond.

In the late 19th and early 20th centuries, entrances to covered bridges were a welcome sight to horses and their drivers. Usually afraid of rushing water, horses would often rear in fright or simply refuse to cross an open bridge. The covered bridge, so like the front of a barn, circumvented this problem.

Some bridges have metal barriers, usually marked with the height and width of the covered bridge, erected in the form of a rectangle just before the entrances on either end of the bridge. These serve to prevent trucks with high loads from ripping out the top of the covered bridges.

On some covered bridge entrances, hand-painted signs or inscriptions enhanced the charm of the bridge. Above the entrance of the Nelson Hollow Bridge is an interesting sign with the inscription, "A $20.00 fine for driving on this bridge Faster Than A Walk."

ST. MARTINS – VAUGHAN CREEK #2

Windows and Walkways

Windows in New Brunswick's covered bridges admit light and add charm to the rustic wooden structures. Some of the bridges have one or two windows while others have more. The openings are in all shapes and sizes. Some of the windows have awnings or roofs and some do not. The awnings were probably designed to reduce the ravishes of the weather which could cause the structure to rot, but for the admirers, they also add to the charm of the structures.

The Hartland Bridge, the longest covered bridge in the world is lighted electrically. The 502 foot St. Nicholas River Number One Bridge (recently burnt down) in Kent County was the other one. It had twelve small rectangular windows extending along its length. Obviously these did not provide sufficient light as a sign warned drivers that lights should be turned on. In the late 1800's and early 1900's travel was by foot or horse and wagon therefore signs warning travellers to turn lights on were not needed.

Many of these structures provide room for single lane traffic only. The importance of headlights in preventing accidents is readily apparent.

Odellach River Number Two Covered Bridge in Victoria County has two interesting windows with awnings, but the Patrick Owens Bridge crossing the Russagonis River in Sunbury County has the most interesting window. It runs almost the entire length of the bridge (over 200 feet) and gives an interesting lighting effect.

Accompanying walkways have been built on two covered bridges in New Brunswick. In 1988 a walkway with slanting roof and windows was built onto the side of the Vaughan Creek Number One Bridge which crosses the Irish River at St. Martins. A tourist or local can now walk in safety to the other side without worrying about vehicular traffic. The walkway also allows the camera buff to stop and snap pictures through the window of the beautiful Bay of Fundy extending out from St. Martins Harbour.

The accompanying walkway attached to the side of Hartland Bridge runs the full length of its 1282 feet. The window openings provide a nice camera shot of the picturesque Saint John River.

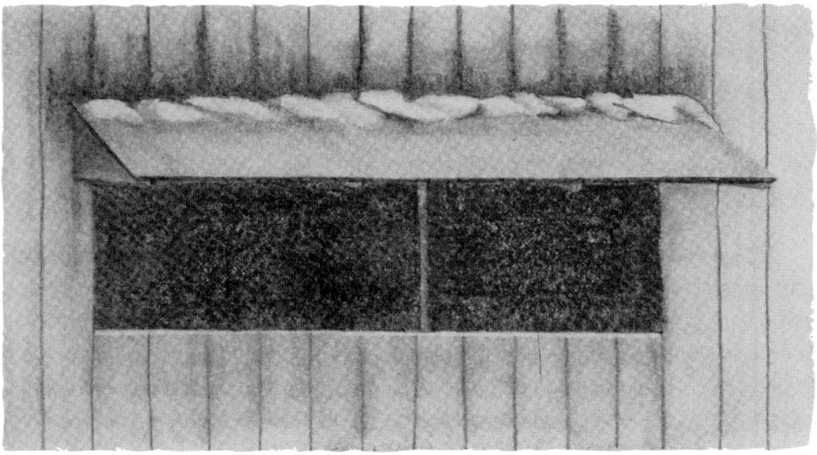

SMALL WINDOW – POINT WOLFE BRIDGE

FULLSIDE WINDOW – RUSAGONIS RIVER #2

Roofs

Covered bridge roofs are an important part of the bridge design and construction. Our forefathers took care and pride in their craftmanship whether in putting a roof on a house or on a covered bridge. New Brunswick's bridges have one of two types of roofs. There is the A-line roof (similar to that on a house) or the Hansard roof (a flatter closed-in roof). The Hansard roof is also sometimes referred to as the cottage or hip roof. Most of New Brunswick's covered bridges incorporated the A-line roof in construction.

There are only two bridges left standing in the province with the Hansard roof, Nelson Hollow in Northumberland County and the Peter Jonah Bridge in Albert County. The latter bridge would have been destroyed in the early 1980's but for prompt action by local residents and the local Albert County Historical Society intent on seeing these bridges preserved as reminders of our past.

Overlapping cedar shingles were used almost exclusively on the covered bridge roofs for 65 years or more. Several of New Brunswick's covered bridges still have their wooden shingles intact like the South Oromocto River Number Two in Sunbury County but most roofs have been updated with asphalt or sheets of steel. The McGuire, McCann, and Dumbarton bridges in Charlotte County all at one time had red asphalt shingles. Today those red asphalt shingles have been replaced by sheet metal roofs.

There is also something unique under the eaves of the roofs of some of New Brunswick's covered bridges. These holes were used to support scaffolding when repairs were necessary. An example of a covered bridge with these is the Bell Bridge crossing the South Oromocto River in Sunbury County.

Map of New Brunswick Showing Counties

To locate New Brunswick Covered Bridges we recommend using The New Brunswick Travel Map which is available free at any New Brunswick Tourism Bureau.

List of Covered Bridges In New Brunswick 2009

The following appendix includes names of bridge, description and location, county, length and year built (when known).

Name	Description and Location	County	Length	Year Built
Weldon Creek No.3 (Hartley Steeves)	Rte. 910 at Salem near Hillsborough	Albert	63' 8"	1923
Coverdale River No. 3 (Bamford Colpitts) (not in service)	Just off Rte. 895 at Colpitts Settlement	Albert	104'10"	1943
Crooked Creek No. 3 (not in service)	Off Rte. 114 on Crooked Creek Rd. near Albert	Albert	93'	1945
Lower Forty Five No. 1	On Barrett Rd. in Fundy National Park	Albert	101'	1914
Point Wolfe	On Point Wolfe Rd. in Fundy National Park	Albert	94'	1992
Saw Mill Creek No. 0.5 (not in service)	Just off Rte. 114 at Hopewell Hill	Albert	105'	1908
Shepody River No. 3 (Germantown)	Just off Rte. 114 at West River Rd.	Albert	61'	1908
Turtle Creek No. 4 (Peter Jonah)	Off Rte. 910 on Peter Jonah Rd.	Albert	64'	1912
William Mitton (not in service)	Near Riverview just off Rte. 112 on Mitton Rd.	Albert	76'	1942

Name	Description and Location	County	Length	Year Built
Becaguimec River No. 3	On Foster Rd. at Mainstream	Carleton	94'8"	1909
Florenceville (One covered span 154' in length)	On Jim Davis Drive off Centreville Rd.	Carleton	950'	1907
Hartland (World's longest covered bridge)	Just off Rte. 2 at Hartland	Carleton	1282'	1921
North Becaguimec River No. 1 (Adair)	On Furlong Rd. one mile north of Cloverdale	Carleton	62'	1948
North Becaguimec River No. 4 (Ellis)	On Howard Brook Rd. one mile north of Carlisle	Carleton	63'	1909

Bridges most recently collapsed, torn down, or lost to fire:
Monquart River No.3 (Keenan) on North Johnville Rd.
North Meduxnekeag No.3 near Weston
Shikatehawk River No.2 on Lockhart Mill Road

Name	Description and Location	County	Length	Year Built
Canal Covered Bridge	On Canal Road just off Rte. 770	Charlotte	123'4"	1917
Dennis Stream No. 3	On Maxwell Crossing Rd. just off Rte. 3	Charlotte	60'	1910

Name	Description and Location	County	Length	Year Built
Digdeguash River No. 3 (McGuire)	Intersection of Rte. 760 and Rioux Rd.	Charlotte	114'9"	1913
Digdeguash River No. 4 (McCann)	On Rte. 770 at Rollingdam	Charlotte	86'	1938
Digdeguash River No. 6 (Dumbarton)	Off Rte. 765 on Tyron Settlement Rd.	Charlotte	76'	1928
Little Lepreau River No. 1.5 (Mill Pond) (not in service)	At Little Lepreau near St. George	Charlotte	104'6"	1910
Magaguadavic River No. 7 (Flume Ridge)	Near Rte. 3 at Flume Ridge on Clark's Mill Pond Road	Charlotte	60'	1905
Acadian Village #1 (replica)	Near Bertrand in Acadian Historical Village	Gloucester		1999
Graham Creek (Tom Graham)	Route 510 West	Kent	135'	1928
Kouchibouguacis No. 5 (Camerons Mill)	Southwest of St. Ignace at Camerons Mill	Kent	136'1/2"	1950

Bridges most recently collapsed, torn down, or lost to fire:

St. Nicholas River No. 1 (Mouth) near Rexton

East St. Nicholas River No. 1 near Rexton

Cocagne River No. 2 at Notre Dame

Name	Description and Location	County	Length	Year Built
Belleisle Creek No. 2 (Marven)	On Swamp Rd. off Rte.124	Kings	71'	1903
Bloomfield Creek	On Bloomfield Station Rd. off Rte. 1	Kings	146'	1917
Darlings Island (not in service)	On Darlings Island Rd. just off Rte. 1 at Nauwigewauk	Kings	137'	1914
Hammond River No. 2 (French Village)	On Rte. 860 at French Village	Kings	181'	1912
Hammond River No. 3 (Smithtown)	On Rte. 860 to Damascus Rd at Smithtown	Kings	182'9"	1914
Kennebecasis River No. 7.5 (Salmon) (not in service)	Off Rte. 890 at Sussex	Kings	112'2"	1908
Kennebecasis River No. 9 (Plumweseep)	On Plumweseep Rd. just off Rte. 1	Kings	74'	1911
Kennebecasis River No. 23 (Malone)	On Goshen Rd. off Rte. 114	Kings	58'	1911
Milkish Inlet No. 1 (Bayswater)	On Kingston Peninsula Rte. 845 at Bayswater	Kings	206'	1920
Millstream No. 5 (Centreville)	On Pleasant Ridge Branch Rd. just off Rte.880 at Berwick	Kings	95'	1911

Name	Description and Location	County	Length	Year Built
Moosehorn Creek No. 1. 5 (not in service)	Just off Rte. 1 near Norton	Kings	94'8"	1915
Smith Creek No. 1 (Tranton)	Just off Rte. 890 on Roachville Rd.	Kings	120'6"	1927
Smith Creek No. 5 (Oldfields)	On Oldfield Rd. off Rte. 890	Kings	92'	1910
Trout Creek No. 4 (Urney)	On Urney Rd. off Waterford Rd. near Sussex	Kings	66'	1905
Trout Creek No. 5 (Moores Mills)	On Drummond Rd. off Waterford Rd. near Sussex	Kings	58'6"	1923
Wards Creek No. 2 (MacFarlane)	Off Rte. 111 on Wards Creek Rd.	Kings	58'	1909
Baker Brook No. 2 (Morneault)	Near Rte. 120 on Cyr St.	Madawaska	94'8"	1939
Green River No. 3 (Boniface)	Off Rte. 2 on Davis Rd. to Boniface Rd.	Madawaska	94'8"	1925

Name	Description and Location	County	Length	Year Built
Quisibis River No. 2	Off Rte. 2 on Deschênes Rd.	Madawaska	55'4"	1951
Nelson Hollow (not in service)	Just off Rte. 8 near Doaktown at Nelson Hollow	Northumberland	80'6"	1900
Canaan River No. 1 (Clark Aaron)	On Cherryvale Rd. off Rte. 112	Queens	164'	1927
Gaspereau River No. 2 (Burpee)	On Cross Rd. at Upper Gaspereau Rd. off Rte.123	Queens	163'6"	1913
Long Creek No. 1 (Starkey)	On Starkey Rd. off Rte. 2	Queens	136'	1939

Bridge recently lost to flooding:
Nerepis River No.3 (Bayard) near Welsford

Tynemouth Creek	Off Rte. 825 on Tynemouth Creek Rd.	Saint John	94'2"	1927
Vaughan Creek No. 1 (Irish River)	At East St. Martins on Bayview Rd.	Saint John	71'6"	1935
Vaughan Creek No. 2 (Hardscrabble)	At East St. Martins on Orange Hill Rd.	Saint John	72'	1946

Name	Description and Location	County	Length	Year Built
Back Creek No. 2 (Hoyt Station)	On Hoyt Station Rd. in Mill Settlement	Sunbury	94'4"	1936
Rusagonis River No. 2 (Patrick Owens)	On Wilsey Rd. off Rte. 655 at Rusagonis	Sunbury	115'6"	1909
South Oromocto River No. 2 (Mill Settlement)	On West Mill Settlement Rd.	Sunbury	136'1/2"	1912
South Oromocto River No. 3 (Bell)	On Boyne Rd. east of Juvenile Settlement	Sunbury	123'4"	1931

Bridges most recently collapsed or torn down
Burpee Millstream No. 2 on Fernmount Road

Name	Description and Location	County	Length	Year Built
Odellach River No. 2 (Tomlinson Mill)	On Rte. 109 at Arthurette	Victoria	60'	1918
Cocagne River No. 3 (Poirier)	Off Rte. 115 on Poirier Office Rd.	Westmorland	136'	1942
Cocagne River No. 5 (Budd)	Off Rte. 126 via Indian Mountain Rd. on Victoria Rd.	Westmorland	83'	1913
Magnetic Hill *Relocation date, originally built in 1915	At Magnetic Hill Park	Westmorland	57'6"	*1983

Name	Description and Location	County	Length	Year Built
Memramcook River No. 4 (Boudreau)	Just off Gayton Rd.	Westmorland	74'	1930
Petitcodiac River No. 3 (Hasty)	Just off Rte. 2 between Petitcodiac and Salisbury	Westmorland	123'4"	1929
Shediac River No. 4 (Joshua Gallant) (not in service)	Cape Breton Rd. onto Shediac River Rd.	Westmorland	84'	1935
Tantramar River No. 2 (Wheaton)	On High Marsh Rd. near Sackville	Westmorland	163'	1916
Eel River No. 3 (Benton)	At Benton on Benton Rd.	York	104'6"	1927
Nackawic River No. 5 (Nackawic Siding)	On Nackawic Siding Rd. between Nackawic and Nortondale	York	63'	

Bridges most recently collapsed, torn down, or lost to fire:
Keswick River No.6 (Stone Ridge) on Upper Stone Ridge Road
Keswick River No. 7 on Haines Siding Rd.
Keswick River No. 8 on Barton Rd.

BIBLIOGRAPHY

Allen, Richard Saunders. Covered Bridges of The Northeast. Revised Edition, The Stephen Breen Press, Brattleboro, Vermont, 1957.

Gillis, John and Stephen. No Faster Than A Walk. Goose Lane Editions, Fredericton, New Brunswick, 1988.

Gregory, Joan. Covered Bridges of New Brunswick. Jil Productions Ltd., Moncton, New Brunswick, 1981.

Harrington, Lyn and Richard. Covered Bridges of Central and Eastern Canada. McGraw Hill Ryerson Ltd., Montreal, 1976.

Joyce, Ronald H. Correspondence: Bridge Department, Province of New Brunswick. Dept. of Transportation, Technical Services Branch, Fredericton, New Brunswick.

Log Book

Bridge	Location	Date

Notes